FOREWORD:

WHAT CAN I WRITE ABOUT BRANT PARKER
THAT HASN'T ALREADY BEEN WRITTEN...
AND WHAT CAN I SAY ABOUT BILL RECHIN
AND DON WILDER THAT HASN'T BEEN SAID.

TO FIND OUT: TAKE EXIT 16 ON THE TACONIC
PARKWAY NORTH AND STOP AT THE FIRST
COMFORT FACILITY.

ONCE INSIDE, ENTER THE DOOR MARKED
"ROOSTERS", AND READ THE WALL IN
THE THIRD STALL TO THE LEFT.

IF YOU ARE AN EMPLOYEE, PLEASE WASH
OUT YOUR MIND BEFORE LEAVING.
IF THIS IS AN INCONVENIENCE TO YOU,
JUST READ THE BOOK.... IT'S PROBABLY
BETTER.

JOHNNY HART

I HATE MONDAYS

by Parker, Rechin
and Wilder

A FAWCETT GOLD MEDAL BOOK • NEW YORK

I HATE MONDAYS

© 1976, 1977, 1978 Field Enterprises, Inc.

© 1978 CBS Publications, the Consumer Publishing Division
of CBS Inc.
A Fawcett Gold Medal Book published by arrangement with
Field Newspaper Syndicate.

ISBN: 0-449-13978-6

Printed in the United States of America

10 9 8 7 6 5 4 3 2 1

tuesday

thursday

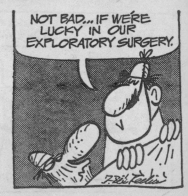

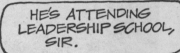

tuesday

tuesday

thursday

saturday

thursday

thursday

Bill Redlin

thursday

tuesday

tuesday

thursday

MORE FUN
FOR THE
LEGIONS OF CROCK FANS

CROCK   1-3868-2 $1.25

AND FROM
THE WIZARD OF ID:

I'M OFF TO SEE THE WIZARD   1-3700-7 $1.25

LONG LIVE THE KING   1-3655-8 $1.25

THE PEASANTS ARE REVOLTING   1-3671-X $1.25

THERE'S A FLY IN MY SWILL   1-3687-6 $1.25

WE'VE GOT TO STOP
  MEETING LIKE THIS   1-3633-7 $1.25